Life in the
HUMAN BODY

Jill Bailey

Chicago, Illinois

D1607234

© 2004 Raintree
Published by Raintree, a division of Reed Elsevier, Inc.
Chicago, Illinois
Customer Service 888-363-4266
Visit our website at www.raintreelibrary.com

For information, address the publisher:
Raintree, 100 N. LaSalle, Suite 1200, Chicago, IL 60602

Project Editors: Geoff Barker, Marta Segal Block, Jennifer Mattson, Tamsin Osler
Production Manager: Brian Suderski
Illustrated by Joanna Williams
Consultant: Michael Chinery
Designed by Ian Winton

Planned and produced by Discovery Books

Library of Congress Cataloging-in-Publication Data:
Bailey, Jill.
Life in the human body / Jill Bailey.
v. cm. -- (Microhabitats)
Includes bibliographical references and index.
Contents: The secret world of humans -- Life in the blood -- From mouth
to gut -- Life on the outside.
ISBN 0-7398-6803-9 (lib. bdg.) ISBN 1-4109-0351-6 (pb)
1. Microorganisms--Juvenile literature. 2. Bacteria--Juvenile
literature. 3. Viruses--Juvenile literature. 4. Body, Human--Juvenile
literature. [1. Microorganisms. 2. Bacteria. 3. Viruses. 4. Body,
Human.] I. Title. II. Series.
QR57.B35 2004
612--dc21
2003006010

Printed and bound in the United States
1 2 3 4 5 6 7 8 9 LB 08 07 06 05 04 03

Acknowledgments
The publishers would like to thank the following for permission to reproduce photographs:
Cover and p.13: Jack Clark/AA/Oxford Scientific Films; p.6: D. Gregory & D. Marshall/Wellcome Photo Library;
p.7: Medical Art Service, Munich/Wellcome Photo Library; p.8: D. Gregory & D. Marshall/Wellcome Photo Library;
p.10: University of Edinburgh/Wellcome Photo Library; p.12: Wellcome Photo Library; p13: Jack Clark/AA/Oxford Scientific
Films; p.14t: Alan Boyde/Wellcome Photo Library; p.14b: D. Gregory & D. Marshall/Wellcome Photo Library; p.15: Scott
Camazine/Oxford Scientific Films; p.16: National Medical Slide Bank/Wellcome Photo Library; p.17: Scott Camazine/
Oxford Scientific Films; p.19: Dr M.I. Walker/Wellcome Photo Library; p.20: Wellcome Photo Library; p.22: Medical Art
Service/Wellcome Photo Library; p.23: Oxford Scientific Films; p.24: Dr John Brackenbury/Science Photo Library; p.25:
University of Edinburgh/Wellcome Photo Library; p.26: Oxford Scientific Films; p.27: Stephen Dalton/Natural History
Photographic Agency; p.28: Oxford Scientific Films; p.29: London Scientific Films/Oxford Scientific Films.

Some words are shown in bold, **like this**. You can find out
what they mean by looking in the glossary.

Contents

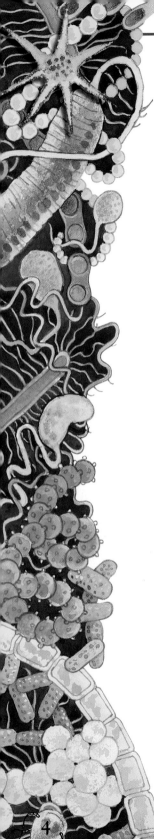

The Body as a Habitat

A Good Home

It might surprise you to find out that the inside of your body is an ideal place for **organisms** to live. It is warm, dark, and moist, and is supplied with plenty of food and oxygen by the blood. There are many possible homes there, such as the mouth and throat; the stomach and **intestines;** and the **windpipe** and lungs. The windpipe is lined with tiny beating hairs, while the intestines are deeply folded. The lungs are full of pockets. These surfaces can provide habitats for many different organisms.

It is perfectly normal for some kinds of organisms to live inside your body. You often do not even notice that they are there, and some of them help you to stay healthy. Other kinds of organisms, however, can make you sick.

Guess What?

If you were able to flatten out the skin of an adult human into a single layer, it would measure about 17.2 to 19.4 sq. ft (1.6 to 1.8 sq. m) in size!

If you smoothed out all the little pockets in the human lungs, they would cover an area about the size of a tennis court.

The outside of your body makes a good home, too. There are cozy places to live between the toes and fingers, under the nails, and even among the hairs on your head. Some organisms live on your skin without harming you at all, while others can cause rashes and other health problems.

The human body is home to a whole world of tiny creatures: bacteria, viruses, fungi, and other organisms.

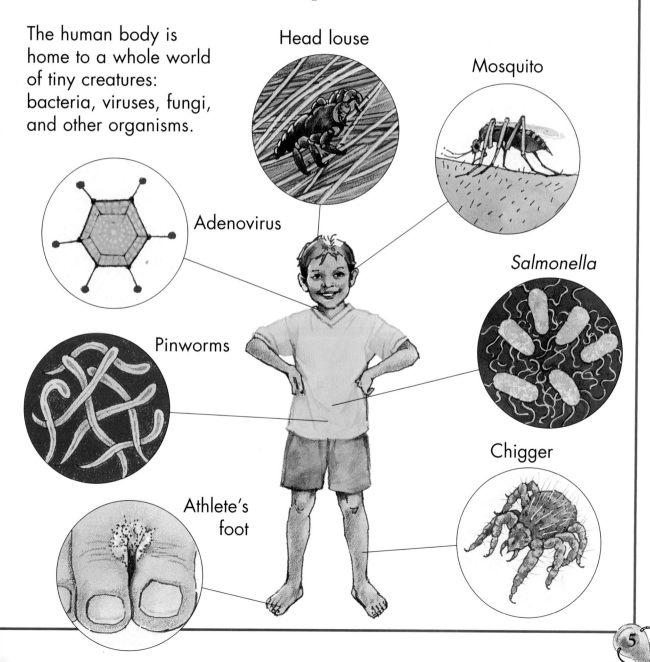

Head louse

Mosquito

Adenovirus

Salmonella

Pinworms

Chigger

Athlete's foot

Invisible Residents

The human body is home to millions of **bacteria** (a single one is called a bacterium) and **viruses.** They are so small that they are invisible to the human eye. One million bacteria would fit on the head of a pin. Viruses are much smaller so millions of them would fit on a pin head.

Our bodies are made up of billions of **cells,** tiny units of living matter. A bacterium is a microscopic **organism** whose body is a single cell. Bacteria ooze juices that dissolve their food. They then absorb the dissolved food all over their bodies. Feeding time for bacteria is like bathing in food.

A highly magnified photograph of bacteria multiplying. Bacteria breed extremely quickly by splitting themselves in two. In just twelve hours, a single bacterium could result in 100 million more.

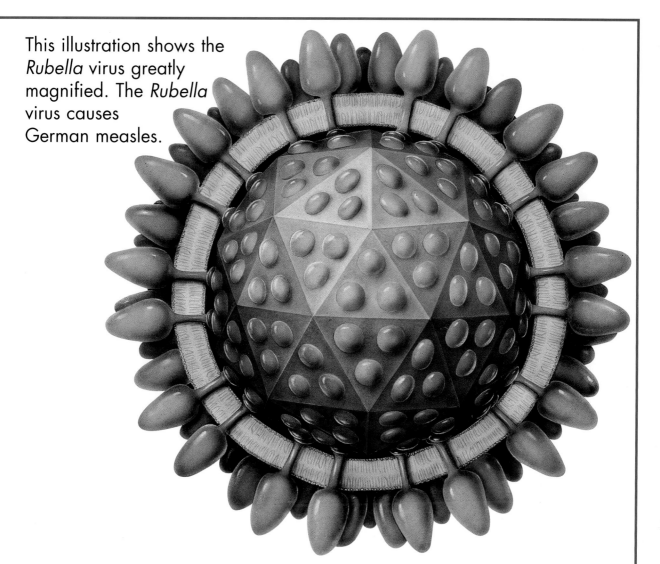

This illustration shows the *Rubella* virus greatly magnified. The *Rubella* virus causes German measles.

Long-distance Travelers

Viruses are not even cells, just chemicals wrapped in thin coats. Many viruses make us ill by injecting their chemicals into the cells of our body and forcing the cells to make new viruses. Then the cells burst and the viruses escape into the blood and travel all over the body, often making us sick. But not all viruses are harmful. Some viruses, known as **bacteriophages,** attack bacteria. They do not attack us.

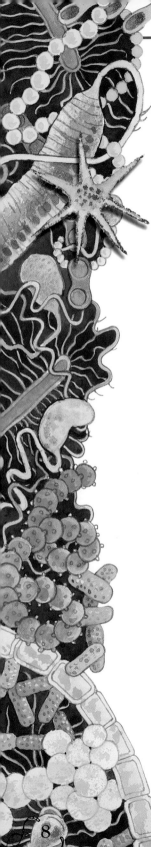

From Outside to Inside

Most of the human body is covered in skin. The only way **bacteria** and **viruses** can get in is through cuts in the skin, or openings such as the eyes, ears, nose, and mouth. The body has many different ways of stopping bacteria and viruses from entering through these openings.

For example, our noses are lined with tiny hairs that trap possible invaders. If bacteria or viruses do get past the hairs, a slimy substance called **mucus** traps them. Hairs and mucus also line the **windpipe** and lungs. Sometimes we cough up the mucus or get rid of it by blowing our noses.

This extremely close-up picture shows the hairs lining the tubes that carry air to and from the lungs. The hairs help to trap harmful dirt and germs.

The eyes and ears also have ways of keeping bacteria out. Our tears wash them away and also contain chemicals to kill them. The wax in our ears makes it difficult for bacteria to get in this way.

Repair Job

One way germs can enter the body is through breaks in the skin. When the skin is pierced by something sharp (1) a net of fine threads forms, trapping red blood cells and blocking the wound (2). In time this hardens into a scab (3). When new skin grows underneath, the scab falls off.

From Inside to Outside

Bacteria and viruses can travel from inside our bodies to the outside, too. This happens when we sneeze or cough, or if we don't wash our hands properly after going to the bathroom.

See for Yourself

Sprinkle some talcum powder on the palm of your hand, then pretend to sneeze or cough over it. Make sure you do this away from other people. Watch the powder fly in all directions. The same thing happens to germs. When you sneeze, air rushes through your nose at a rate of over 100 mi (160 km) an hour. That can expel bacteria and viruses a long way. So cover your mouth and nose when you cough or sneeze, and keep your germs to yourself.

9

Life in the Blood

A Warm Home

Blood travels around the body in blood vessels, or long, narrow tubes called **arteries** and **veins,** and a network of smaller tubes called **capillaries** that connect the arteries and veins. The heart pumps blood along the arteries to all parts of the body. Blood returns to the heart through the veins. The inside of a blood vessel is a dark, warm place, through which blood pushes through in surges, or pulses.

Blood is a watery liquid containing dissolved food and oxygen. Different kinds of cells float in the blood. **Red blood cells** carry oxygen from the lungs to the rest of the body. Living things need oxygen to burn up their food and release energy. **White blood cells** fight infections, while fragments of cells called **platelets** help stop bleeding.

Red blood cell

A highly-magnified electron microscope photograph of blood. Red blood cells look like sausages when seen in side view.

White blood cell

Defending the Body

The blood cells are some of the body's most important defenses. Large white blood cells called **macrophages** actually eat up bacteria, while other white cells make them stick together in clumps so they cannot work properly. White cells also produce chemicals that make safe the harmful chemicals released by the **bacteria.**

Red blood cell

Macrophage

Bacteria

A macrophage (here colored yellow) swallows up a bacterium.

Guess What?

The human body contains about 8 pt (4.5 l) of blood.

If all the body's blood vessels were placed end-to-end, they would measure over 62,000 mi (nearly 100,000 km).

Every second 15 million blood cells are destroyed in the human body, but they are all replaced.

As it travels through the body, each red blood cell will cover about 300 mi (480 km) before it wears out and dies.

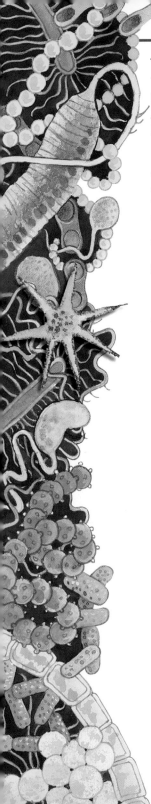

Body Invaders

Our **arteries** and **veins** provide homes not only for **bacteria** and **viruses,** but also for other small invaders.

Many **organisms** that cause illness are passed to humans through insect bites. The tiny, one-celled creature called a trypanosome that causes sleeping sickness is carried by the tsetse fly. Certain mosquitoes in tropical countries spread the virus that causes yellow fever.

Plague is a serious disease caused by a bacterium mainly carried by the fleas that live on rats. If an infected flea bites a human, it can pass on the plague bacterium. The disease spreads very quickly. Seven hundred years ago it killed about 25 million people in Europe and Asia. Cases of plague still occasionally occur today.

During the great plague of London in the 1600s, thousands of people died.

World's Worst Killer?

Every twelve seconds someone dies from **malaria.** Malaria is a serious illness that is most common in Africa. It is caused by a kind of **plasmodium,** a small, single-celled organism, which spends part of its life in a mosquito, and part of its life in a person. When a mosquito infected by plasmodia bites a human, lots of plasmodia enter the body.

The plasmodia multiply in the body, first in the liver and then in the blood, over and over again. The infected human suffers bursts of fever and shivering. When a mosquito that is not infected with plasmodia bites a human suffering from malaria, it picks up the plasmodia and can pass them on to another person.

Male mosquitoes sip nectar from flowers but the females feed on blood. The female's body swells with blood as she feeds. She needs blood to make her eggs.

Life Inside the Body

From Mouth to Intestine

The food we eat passes from the throat to the stomach and down a long swiggly tube, the **intestine,** where it is **digested** and absorbed. The intestine is an ideal place for **organisms**—warm, wet, and full of food. Fine fingers of flesh, called **villi,** stick out into the intestines. They contain tiny blood vessels called **capillaries** that absorb food.

This close-up photograph shows the villi in the human intestine.

Millions of **bacteria** live in the intestines. Some help us by digesting things we ourselves cannot digest, and by making vitamins that keep us healthy. Others attack bacteria that might be harmful. Different kinds of bacteria live in different parts of the intestine. There are other single-celled creatures there too, feeding on the bacteria.

The *Giardia,* a single-celled organism, attaches itself to the side of the intestine. It can cause stomach aches.

Enemy Bacteria

Sometimes harmful bacteria are found in the intestine. *Salmonella* and *Escherichia coli* (commonly called *E. coli*) are bacteria that can cause food poisoning. *Helicobacter* may cause stomach **ulcers.**

Our bodies have some defenses against these bacteria. Some are trapped in our **esophagus,** the tube that leads from the throat to the stomach, while the stomach itself contains a strong **acid** that kills most bacteria that enter it.

Guess What?

If the many folds and twists of your intestine were straightened out, it would be about 26 ft (8 m) long.

An average American eats over 50 tons (50,000 kg) of food, and drinks more than 13,000 gal (over 49,000 l) of liquid in a lifetime.

Your stomach has to make a new lining every two weeks or it would digest itself.

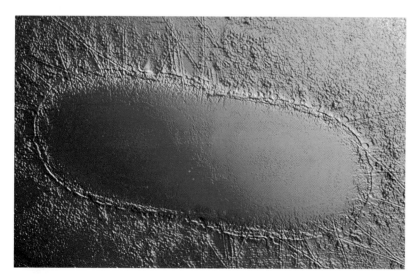

A close-up view, colored by the computer, of the bacterium *E. coli*. It feeds on sugars contained in the food we eat.

Life on Tongue and Tooth

The spaces between teeth fill with food at every meal or snack, and are ideal homes for **bacteria** and other tiny **organisms.** They live in a slimy **mucus** between the teeth, forming a layer called plaque. These bacteria feed on sugary foods, and then produce **acids** that eat into the teeth, causing decay. The acids eventually get washed down the throat by saliva, produced by glands around the mouth to help food slip down the throat. Brushing your teeth helps to get rid of any acid left behind. But if you keep snacking between meals, there is always a fresh supply of sugar and acid to damage the teeth.

You can avoid teeth like these— and toothache—by brushing your teeth after meals, and not eating too many sugary snacks.

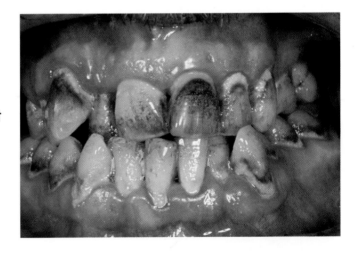

Fungi (one is called a fungus) live on the teeth, too, especially **yeasts,** which also like sugary foods. Fungi are simple organisms that feed by oozing juices on their food to digest it, then soaking it up.

Sore Mouths

Bacteria and **viruses** can give you illnesses and unpleasant sores in and around the mouth. Cold sores and mouth **ulcers** are usually caused by viruses. Some bacteria that live on the tongue can sometimes lead to illness. Some *Streptococcus* bacteria and **adenoviruses** give you sore throats, while others attack the **tonsils,** causing tonsillitis. But most of the time, it is the tonsils that attack the bacteria, producing chemicals to destroy them.

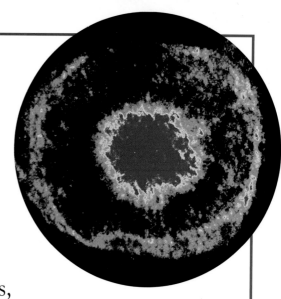

This brightly-colored computer image shows the virus that causes cold sores on the mouth.

See for Yourself

Ask permission from a grown-up to let you put four raw eggs into four glasses. Cover each egg with a different liquid: milk, tea, water, and cola. Watch what happens over several days. The eggshells react in the same way as your teeth. What happens if you try to clean them with a toothbrush and toothpaste?

Buy some plaque-disclosing tablets from a drugstore. If you follow the instructions on the packet your teeth will become stained, showing where there are bacteria.

17

Parasitic Worms

Parasites are animals that feed and live on another animal, usually without killing it. The tapeworm is a parasite that can infect humans, where it lives in the **intestines.** It is long and flat, with a very thin skin through which it absorbs its liquid food—which we have **digested** for it—all over its body. When the tapeworm sheds its eggs, they pass out with undigested food. In places that lack good sewer systems, the eggs may get into soil and streams, and infect farm animals feeding or drinking there. Humans then become infected by eating their meat.

Tail

Head

A tapeworm uses a ring of hooks on its head to cling to the wall of the intestines.

Other kinds of parasitic worms, such as the *Ascaris* worm and pinworm, may also live in our intestines. They lay their eggs in places they can easily get to, such as seats, towels, and clothes. They can also get under your fingernails, so you should always wash your hands before eating.

Flat Flukes

Flukes are flat worms, one fifth of an inch (5 millimeters) to four inches (100 millimeters) long. Some live in the blood, and others in the liver or other organs. Their eggs pass out of the body in the urine of an infected person. If the eggs end up in river water, they may enter humans through their mouth when they swim in that river. Flukes can also burrow through the skin of people fishing or working in flooded rice fields. They infect millions of people in Africa and east Asia.

Guess What?

There are over 3,000 different kinds of tapeworms.

The longest worm that infects human beings is the fish tapeworm. It can grow to more than 30 ft (10 m) in length!

The beef tapeworm produces about 2,500,000,000 eggs in its lifetime.

The *Ascaris* worm can grow up to 9 in. (22.5 cm) long, and be as thick as a pencil.

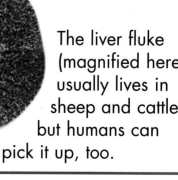

The liver fluke (magnified here) usually lives in sheep and cattle, but humans can pick it up, too.

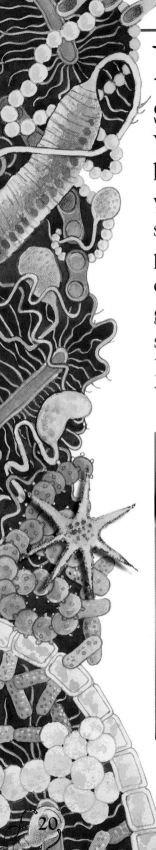

Life Outside the Body

Surface Dwellers

You cannot see them, but there are millions of harmless **bacteria** and probably some **fungi** living on your skin. The skin is food for many tiny creatures, such as the ringworm fungus, which causes scaly patches on the skin or blisters. Other kinds of fungi cause athlete's foot and diaper rash. Bacteria that get below the skin surface through tiny cuts and sores can cause boils and nastier diseases like leprosy, which affects the skin and nerves. **Viruses** can cause warts as well as cold sores.

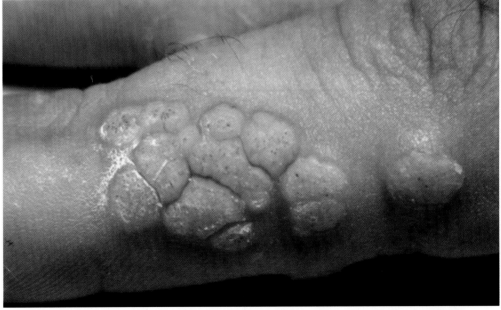

This picture shows a bad case of warts on a finger. Warts are caused by viruses that live in the skin.

Dust Eaters

Bits of skin rub off all the time and are replaced by new skin. The dead skin we shed is food for dust mites that live in our houses. Dust mites usually live in bedding and carpets but they may also hide in folds of our skin and among our hairs. Too small to see without a microscope, they clean up the dustlike bits of skin we leave behind us. Some people have an allergy, or bad reaction, to the droppings of dust mites. Their allergy may bring on asthma attacks.

Without dust mites, our houses would be full of a fine powder made up of tiny flakes of skin.

Guess What?

An adult human sheds about 600,000 tiny pieces of skin every hour.

Most people shed about 110 lb (50 kg) of skin in a lifetime.

We replace our outer skin cells about every 27 days—that makes almost 1,000 new skins in a lifetime.

Biters, Burrowers, and Suckers

Mites are minute, eight-legged animals. Some kinds of mites feed on blood rather than skin. They have sharp **mouthparts** that pierce the skin and suck out blood. As they feed, these mites inject chemicals into the skin that cause intense itching. Female mites burrow into the skin to lay their eggs. Most mites pass from human to human by contact with skin or clothing.

This painting shows a mite crawling through the skin. You can see her eggs in the burrow behind her.

The young of certain kinds of mites are known as chiggers. Chiggers burrow into the skin. They often live in grassy areas, and crawl up the socks of a passing person to reach bare skin.

A Lousy Time

Head lice live in hair. They have strong, curved claws for clinging to strands of hair. They feed on blood in the scalp, and glue their eggs to hairs in sacs called nits. The eggs rub off onto clothing, and easily pass from one person to another. Louse bites, too, become itchy.

Body lice and crab lice lay their eggs in clothing and bedding. Both mites and lice may carry unwelcome **bacteria** and **viruses.** Some of these can cause serious diseases. The droppings of the body louse can carry *rickettsiae*, the tiny **parasitic organisms** that cause the disease typhus.

A head louse holds onto hair with its claws. It prefers clean hair because it is easier to cling to than greasy hair.

Little Visitors

Many small animals visit humans from time to time to feed on our skin, our sweat, or our blood. These visitors find us by our smell, by the heat our bodies give off, or by the carbon dioxide gas we breathe out.

Butterflies, sweat flies, and sweat bees need to eat salty substances to survive. They can get the salt they need by sipping sweat. If you leave a pair of sweaty socks around in the tropics, you may return to find butterflies sipping from them!

These butterflies are drinking sweat from a walker's socks. Sweat contains both salt and water, which the butterflies need in their diet.

This photo shows what a tick's spiky mouthparts (in the center of this picture) look like when highly magnified by an electron microscope.

Eight-legged Blood Suckers

Ticks are small creatures with hard bodies and eight little legs. They feed on many animals, including humans, by sucking up blood. Ticks have jagged **mouthparts** that are like the teeth of a saw. The teeth point backwards, so it is very difficult to remove a tick from the skin. When a tick is pulled from the body, the mouthparts tend to break off and remain in the skin.

Bugs that Bite

Bedbugs are insects with flat, hard bodies that can sneak into crevices or cracks in walls and beds, or into the folds of bedding. They come out at night to feed on humans and other warm-blooded animals such as mice. In less than five minutes a bedbug can drink enough blood to last it until its next meal. It usually feeds again after a week, but it can survive for up to six months without food.

A bedbug swells up as it sucks blood from human skin.

Bedbugs thrive where bedding is not washed very often, and where there is old furniture, peeling wallpaper, bare floorboards, and lots of places to hide. The females lay up to 200 eggs, which they glue to wood, cloth, or paper.

High Jumpers

Fleas are also blood-sucking **parasites.** Different types of fleas live on different mammals, including humansand birds. Human fleas used to be quite common when humans did not bathe as often as we do today.

Both the cat flea and the dog flea are likely to be the cause of most flea bites on humans today. Their bites produce a raised red mark that irritates the skin and is very itchy.

Fleas do a somersault as they jump through the air, with their legs and claws stretched out and ready to grab hold of their victim.

Leeches—Friend and Foe

Leeches make life uncomfortable for people in tropical rain forests. They feed on both cold-blooded animals, such as fish and snails, and on warm-blooded animals, including humans. A leech is like a short, fat worm with a sucker at each end. It has three jaws with sharp teeth that cut a Y-shaped hole in the flesh. As it bites it injects an **anesthetic** and a chemical to prevent the victim's blood thickening and clotting to seal up the wound.

A bloated leech full of human blood. Its body stretches as it feeds.

In medicine leeches have been used for centuries to treat all sorts of human diseases. Today medical leeches are used in hospitals to remove excess fluid from patients during plastic surgery. They are also used to help keep the blood flowing and stop it from clotting after sewing back severed fingers or toes.

The Good and the Bad

Not all **organisms** that live in and on the human body are bad for us. Some **bacteria** do us more good than harm, while many other visiting creatures only cause problems for a short time. Really harmful intruders are not common, except in the tropics or where people have a shortage of clean drinking water or live in dirty, crowded conditions. But even in the cleanest of surroundings, if you do not wash your hands before meals, after going to the bathroom, and after playing outside, you may pick up a little traveler that you do not want.

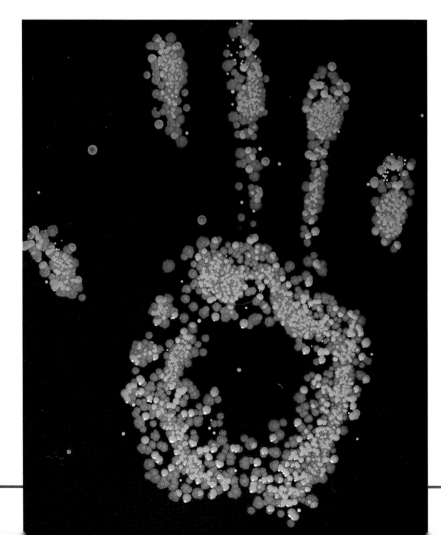

The blotches on this handprint are bacteria. Bacteria on a hand were left on a handprint where they rapidly multiplied to become visible colonies.

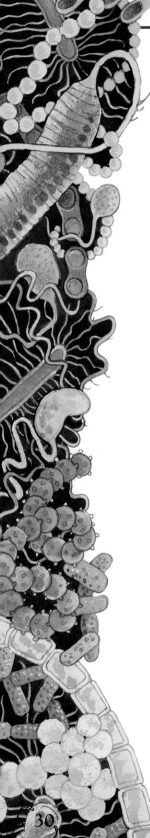

Glossary

acid chemical substance that is sour compared with water

adenovirus group of viruses that causes infections of the nose, the throat, the tonsils, and the eyes

anesthetic chemical substance that stops you feeling pain

artery tube that carries blood from the heart to the rest of the body

bacteriophage virus that attacks bacteria

bacterium (plural—bacteria) microscopic organism (too small to be seen without a microscope) that is just a single cell with a stiff or flexible cell wall. Bacteria absorb food from their surroundings and multiply by simply dividing in two.

capillary tiny, branching blood vessel found at the tip of an artery

cell smallest unit of living material in an organism

digest to break down and absorb food

esophagus tube that leads from the throat to the stomach

fungus (plural—fungi) living organism made up of many cells, arranged like branching threads, or single cells, as in yeast. The fungus feeds by producing digestive juices to dissolve its food, then absorbing that liquid food through the surface of its body.

intestine tube through which food passes to be digested. In humans it includes the esophagus, the stomach, the small intestine (where food is digested and absorbed), and the larger intestine (which absorbs water and makes the waste solid).

macrophage large white blood cell that attacks bacteria and other invading organisms by swallowing them up

malaria disease spread by mosquitoes that causes high fever and chills, and weakness

mouthparts structures around the mouth, which are used to pick up or eat food. They may be like tiny jaws, or they may form a tube or sucker.

mucus slimy substance found in the nose, throat, and other parts of the body

organism any living creature

plasmodium (plural—plasmodia) single-celled parasite that causes malaria

platelet special kind of cell fragment found in the blood. Platelets clump together to help form blood clots to seal wounds.

red blood cell cell in the blood that carries oxygen around the body

tonsils two lumps of tissue, or mass of cells, at the back of the throat, which help to fight infection. Food sometimes gets stuck in tiny cavities in the tonsils, or the tonsils themselves become infected with bacteria causing them to swell up and hurt (tonsillitis).

ulcer open sore that does not heal. Ulcers commonly get infected because the skin is broken, so germs can get to the tissues below.

vein tube that carries blood from various parts of the body toward the heart

villi finger-like growths from the linings of the intestines. Villi contain tiny blood vessels called capillaries that carry the food away.

virus extremely tiny organism, much smaller than a bacterium, that is made up of a core of chemicals wrapped in a protein coat

white blood cell cell in the blood that is involved in the defense against germs

windpipe tube that connects the throat to the lungs

yeast kind of fungus that is usually made up of just one cell

Further Reading

Farndon, John. *The Human Body*. Chicago: Raintree, 2001.

Fredericks, Anthony D. *Bloodsucking Creatures*. New York: Scholastic Library Publishing, 2002.

Royston, Angela. *Head Lice*. Chicago: Heinemann, 2002.

Snedden, Robert. *The Benefits of Bacteria*. Chicago: Heinemann, 2000.

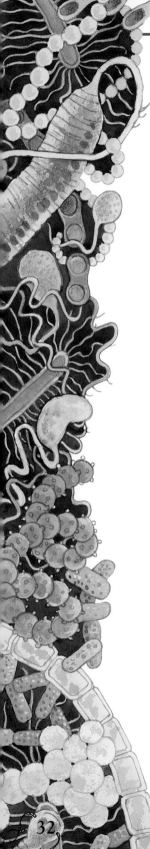

Index